245+ Christmas Tips for Frugal Moms

by: Lara Velez, Founder of **Moms of Faith**

I0159463

Credits:

Cover Art: *istock.com*

Copyright © AliBelle, LLC All Rights Reserved

Copyright © AliBelle, LLC, All Rights Reserved

Table of Contents

Copyright © AliBelle, LLC, All Rights Reserved

Introduction

Our family has had many times throughout the years that our budget had to be very tight around Christmas. I have had to learn to be creative and frugal. I wrote this book to share these ideas with you!

I have a ton of tips and ideas to help you have an affordable Christmas, as well as find fun and... CHEAP things to do with your family!

In this book you will not only find frugal gift ideas, and age-appropriate ideas, you will also find many money saving tips, and tons of activities to do during the Christmas season that are free, inexpensive and fun to do as a family! This book is FILLED with ideas that will not break the bank during the holiday season!

Note: I tried not to repeat myself, however, in the kids' gift idea chapter there may be a couple repeats.

Copyright © AliBelle, LLC, All Rights Reserved

Frugal Gift Ideas

Giving does not have to mean that every year you rack up credit card debt or stress out about what to get who and how much to spend on so and so. If you are creative and think outside the box, you can find that there are MANY gifts that are free or extremely cheap.

Here are my frugal gift ideas...

Bake. This is a great way to get the kids involved as well. Bake some cookies, cupcakes, or make a yummy candy. Buy some inexpensive colored cellophane and tie it up pretty–or use paper lunch bags, wrapping paper, colorful tins, or whatever is inexpensive and available to you. You can find TONS of wrapping options at the dollar store.

Use your talents. It's FREE! If you are great at organizing, give the gift of a few hours to a friend to help them get organized in an area of their home. If you knit, make something special for someone on your list. If you are great with taxes, offer to do them for a friend or loved one. Sky is the limit with this one.

Homemade Gifts. Grandma and Grandpa are sure to love a hand made gift over a store bought one

Copyright © AliBelle, LLC, All Rights Reserved

from their little love bugs. It is also a great idea for us Moms too! A few ideas…

> *knit, sew, crochet - You can make blankets, scarves, mittens, napkins, etc.*

> *scrapbook- You can create a photo collage, a special memory scrapbook, etc.*

> *woodwork – You can design some napkin rings, cross, keepsake box, etc.*

> *jewelry – This is a great idea for those who have this ability. Make a beaded necklace, earring, etc.*

> *potpourri - You can make your own with different spices and scented oils.*

> *bath salts - create you own homemade jars of bath salts and soaps.*

> *Be Creative! You can do SO much if you just get those creative juices flowing and USE your God given talents!*

Acts of Random Kindness. Pay for the person's toll, fast food meal, etc. behind you. Help someone put their groceries in the car. Offer to go grocery shopping for an elderly person. Get creative with

Copyright © AliBelle, LLC, All Rights Reserved

kindness and it is sure to spread around and maybe even come back around your way!

iTunes. Purchase a $5-$10 iTunes gift card for the music lover in your life.

Calendar. Have a friend that loves kittens? Get her a calendar with cute kittens for each month. This works for ANY person…golfer, fisher, Precious Moments, cows, etc. You know what your family and friends like. This is a cheap…yet personal gift!

Make a Coupon Book. This is always fun. Create a special book of things you will do for someone on your list. What you put in the book really depends on who the gift is for. However, here are a few ideas: back massage (hubbie would love this), clean house, hug, lunch, spa day, an hour of your time, etc.

Something Old. Re-gift something you received that you have not opened and most likely will not use in the next 100 years. NO there is NOTHING wrong with re-gifting! Especially if money is tight. Just don't re-gift to the one who got you the gift! Um…Awkward!

Nuts. They sell these in bulk, bags and in cans. You can create your own pretty jar, bag, etc. Nuts are a yummy, inexpensive and nice gift to give.

Copyright © AliBelle, LLC, All Rights Reserved

Recipe in a Bag. Do you have a cookie, cake, sauce, pasta or bread recipe that people love? Put all the dry ingredients in a pretty bag/jar with a recipe card of what else they need and how to make it!

Family Pics. Grandparents love pictures as gifts. If you can get your pictures made, do that and put it in a pretty frame. Otherwise, take them yourself, develop and put them in a pretty frame. Either way, the grandparents are sure to love them!

Green Thumb. This is for the gardener in your life...give a plant, flower, tree, pot with seeds, or even gardening tools. You can take it one step further and decorate a pretty pot for them. Then, plant something pretty in it that they can nurture and grow!

Books. I love books and so do many of my friends. Most books are affordable–especially if you shop Amazon or an online book store. Even ebooks make GREAT gifts these days! Many are under $5 & $10! **Most of my books are under a buck!**

Gas Card. We all know gas prices are not going to be dropping any time soon–if ever! A gas card can be an AWESOME gift to give!

I Love You Because... Fill a jar, gift bag or decorative box with a bunch of notes telling all the reasons you love or appreciate the receiver.

Copyright © AliBelle, LLC, All Rights Reserved

Flash Drive. They sell these for less then 10 bucks. Many have cool designs on them as well. This would be a wonderful gift for the techie in your life.

Freebies. Use your free offers as gifts. Let's say you buy a body lotion and you get one free. Give the free one to someone else. Two gifts in one. You can do this with all 'free with purchase' offers. It is a great way to stock up as well. Save all your freebies throughout the year, and you will have a stash of "go to" presents to help keep you on budget!

Journal. I love journals. This is a frugal gift idea for the writer in your life. You can find them anywhere for $3-$10. Be sure and write a heartfelt note to add a special touch to it!

Collage. This is a great idea for a close friend, relative, Mom or daughter. Create a collage using pictures, memories, and things they love. It is sure to bring some loving tears to the receiver's eyes.

Gift Basket. This can go in just about any direction…crafty, cookies, fruit, sweets, hobby related, spa, movie night, fun, etc.

Coffee Mug. Do you have a coffee or mug lover on your list? Buy a nice mug and a bag of their

Copyright © AliBelle, LLC, All Rights Reserved

favorite coffee. This is also a great tip for a tea lover or hot cocoa fan!

Bath and Body Works. They have HUGE sales. You can get 5 lotions or fancy sanitizers for $20 many times throughout the year. That's FIVE gifts! Wrap it up pretty with a personal card and it is a sure winner!

Pet lovers. You can get treats, new leash, pet bed, grooming, etc.

It's OK to be Practical. Not all gifts need to be knock your socks off original. Try buying a hair cut, socks, mani/pedi, stamps, computer paper, ink, groceries, etc. Be creative in your practicality! LOL!

Herb Garden. This is a winner for the cook in your life. Herb gardens are cheap and they do not take up a lot of space.

Deck of Cards. If there is a card lover in your life, buy them a deck of cards. Then, Google card games and rules. Print out the rules and give them with the cards. Or, if you have a few extra bucks, buy a card game rule book to go with the cards.

The Entertainment® Coupon Book. This is an GREAT gift to give someone. You can get it from your kid's school many times or just go to entertainment.com.

Copyright © AliBelle, LLC, All Rights Reserved

Time. Nothing says, "I care" more than your time. You can make a coupon gift, take a friend to lunch, organize a room in your friend's house. Whatever your talent is, give it to someone. It costs you nothing but your time and THAT is the best gift you can give.

Edible Goodies. This can go in so many directions. Cook for someone. Bake cookies and put them in decorative tins you can get at the dollar store. Make jar gifts with the dry ingredients and recipe of your favorite cookies, brownies, etc.

Pedicure. This is less then $20 and I know BOTH sexes like this!

Gift Cards. These are great gifts when you have no time, or for parties. $10 is not a bad gift card. Trust me, the person will NOT give it back! LOL!

Music. Create a CD of your friend or loved one's favorite songs. If it is for a spouse, make a LOVE CD.

Ornament. You can buy or design a pretty ornament.

Stationary. This is always a sure thing with a woman.

Copyright © AliBelle, LLC, All Rights Reserved

Gourmet Coffee or Teas. Again, you can find these in grocery stores. Instead of going to a specialty shop where you will spend too much money, buy them at the grocery store and make the presentation creative.

Costco/Sams Club Membership. There are several great places like these that offer the buyer an inexpensive alternative. Yes, it is bulk shopping, however, we did the math and we really do save money. This is a great gift for about $50 (or less) and it will last a whole year!

Movie Night. Buy a $5 BlockBuster gift card, large microwave movie theatre popcorn bowl, and candy. Put it in the popcorn container and there you have a gift that anyone will appreciate.

Beauty Supplies. Look for sales. Buy one get one free lotions are very popular this time of year. Use it to your advantage and you can have two gifts for the price of one.

Framed Picture. This is the perfect gift for a parent or loved one. Frame a picture you know they will appreciate. They will LOVE it!

Candy Jar. This is a nice gift for the chocolate lover in your life. You can find an inexpensive and pretty jar just about anywhere. Fill it with Hershey kisses, tootsie rolls or some other favorite sweet treat.

Copyright © AliBelle, LLC, All Rights Reserved

Acronym. Create an acronym for a special person. My daughter loves to do this and I have done it for a few friends. It is a special gift that takes time and effort. However, it is worth it! You will take each letter of their first name and come up with a nice word that describes them. Make it pretty and creative too!

Example: for the name Pam –

Positive

Adorable

Mindful.

Date Night. Make a decorative "certificate" that states the bearer will receive one (or more) free child watching services. Basically, you will watch a friend or family member's kids so they can have a night off!

As Seen On TV. My husband LOVES these items! LOL! They actually have an "As Seen On TV" store in a local mall in our town. You can also find many at Target. They are cheap and cool gifts!

Candles. Who doesn't love candles??

Make a Meal. Give a loved one the night off! This is a fabulous way to share a bit of you with

Copyright © AliBelle, LLC, All Rights Reserved

someone…Make them one of your signature recipes and take it over for them to enjoy with their family. You can make it so they can freeze it, or plan ahead so they know to be ready for it.

Starbucks. Even a $5 gift card will make someone on your list smile. I know I would love you forever! LOL! Five bucks is good for one fabulous cup of yumminess!

Magazine subscription. Buy a one year subscription for a friend/family member's favorite magazine, or hobby magazine you think they would enjoy!

Fuzzy Socks. We love fuzzy socks. You can find them at Target, Walmart–pretty much anywhere! They are fuzzy and have cool designs. Very fun and frugal gift! (this is a great gift for girls of all ages)

Next chapter are cheap gift ideas for your children and teenagers…

Copyright © AliBelle, LLC, All Rights Reserved

Great Kid Gift Ideas

Some of these inexpensive gift ideas can be used for multiple ages. That is why you may see the same idea more than once with a different twist in some cases!

All Kids...

Time. Time is important to your kids. Make them a special coupon book of things you know they would like to do. Or make a "gift certificate" of a special day you plan and present it to them. They will have it to look forward to in the near future.

Toddlers...

Balls. Toddlers are easy to please. Balls are fun and teach eye hand coordination.

Dress Up Clothes. You do not have to spend a fortune on a store bought dress up outfit! Go to your local thrift store, give some pretty hand me downs, or clear your closet. They will LOVE dressing up.

Copyright © AliBelle, LLC, All Rights Reserved

Puzzles. Great gifts for little ones. Many times, you can find these at the dollar section at Target, or even the dollar store.

Books. Buy them a book and READ it to them.

Play Dough. My kids LOVED play dough and it is non toxic, so this is a great and inexpensive gift for toddlers and even a little older.

Children 5-10...

Dress Up Clothes. Older kids like to play dress up too.

Candy. This is a no-brainer.

Board Game. Games are fun. PLAY the games with them.

Books. Buy them their favorite book or a few in their favorite series.

Diary. Encourage them to write their feelings.

Coloring Books and Crayons. Most kids love to color.

Hot Wheels. My husband loves these. LOL!

Copyright © AliBelle, LLC, All Rights Reserved

Stuffed Animals. Who doesn't love stuffed animals?

Barbies. Great gift for a girl and MANY of them are $10 and under.

Slippers. Kids love character slippers. Pay Less sells them for cheap.

Jump Rope. Easy and great gift to get them moving.

Figurines. This is a good one for girls or boys. My daughter loves horses, and I have gotten her inexpensive horse figurines, and she loves them!

Copyright © AliBelle, LLC, All Rights Reserved

Tweens and Teens...

Gift Cards. Teenagers LOVE to shop. This is a GREAT gift for a boy or girl.

Disposable Cell Phone. If you cannot afford a cell phone, get them a disposable one. At least they will get it for a bit and it will encourage them to work for it! It will also let you know if they are ready for the responsibility.

CD's/iTunes/Music. Music is a no-brainer. Be careful what you put in their ears though!

Books. If they like to read, get them their favorite type of book.

Journals. They need to have a place to vent and put their feelings

Pens. I know girls love these.

Craft Supplies. If they are crafty or good with their hands, this is a fun gift.

Models. A lot of boys like to create models. Airplanes, boats, etc...

Pedicure. This is less then $20 and I know BOTH sexes like this! LOL!

Sports. Get them a poster of their favorite sports person. Or, anything related to sports!

Party. Create a coupon or certificate agreeing to throw a slumber or regular party for them and be the hostess with the mostest.

Video Games. You can find inexpensive games at garage sales and places that offer trades and sell used games. Trust me; most kids couldn't care less if the game is new.

Clothes. Obviously, getting clothes is not necessarily the only thing that should be under the tree. However, one or two outfits or shirts would not fall into the eye roll category.

Magazine Subscription. Most magazine subscriptions are fairly inexpensive. They range from $10-$25.

Beauty Bag. This can be all done at a dollar store, or the dollar sections at Walmart/Target. Get a cute inexpensive cosmetic bag and add some nail polish, samples, eye shadow and other inexpensive beauty items. Fabulous idea for the teenage girl in your life! Most teenage girls LOVE anything related to beauty.

Copyright © AliBelle, LLC, All Rights Reserved

Stocking Stuffer Ideas

For our family, the stocking stuffers are the best part, because, just when you think you are done, there is still a fabulous stocking filled with goodies. Below you will find over 100 stocking stuffer ideas. However, feel free to use the ideas as inexpensive gifts ideas too!

Stocking Stuffer Ideas for Her

- Hair accessories
- Bath accessories – body lotion, loofah etc.
- Cosmetics (eye shadow, tweezers, nail polish, applicators, lip gloss, etc)
- Scented soap
- Perfume
- Jewelry – bracelet, earrings, rings, charms to add to a bracelet or necklace
- Small diary or journal
- Pens, pencils, erasers
- Herbal tea sachets
- Magnets
- Cell phone cover
- Chocolate
- Starbucks gift card
- Sticky Notes
- Mini flashlight
- Votive candles and/or holders

Copyright © AliBelle, LLC, All Rights Reserved

- Pretty compact mirror
- Personal safety alarm
- Mittens/Gloves
- Temporary Tattoos
- Craft supplies
- Wristlet, small purse
- Desk items
- Book from favorite author
- Pretty scarf
- Magazine subscription
- Digital photo frame
- Gym membership
- Pocket planner (you can find these little 1-2 year calendars in the Target dollar section!)

Stocking Stuffer Ideas for Him

- Disposable razor or refills
- Travel toiletries – shaving kit
- Small pocket knife
- Golf tees
- Golf balls
- Fishing tackle
- Sport themed small item
- Bowling towel (small towel for wiping bowling ball)
- Cologne
- Gift Card
- Event tickets
- Back scrubber
- Soap on a Rope

Copyright © AliBelle, LLC, All Rights Reserved

- Watch
- Book light
- Tools
- Magazine subscriptions
- Tire gauge
- Travel mug
- Photo mouse pad
- Alarm clock
- Wallet
- Cuff links
- Tie
- Calculator
- Bike lock
- Gym membership

Stocking Stuffer Ideas for Kids *(various ages)*

(Note: it is to the parent's discretion what gifts are appropriate for their child's age, maturity, etc. Please use caution and common sense.)

- Candy
- Kelly dolls (small Barbie type dolls for like $5)
- Hot wheels (boys love these little cars…er…husbands too!)
- Target dollar section (they have TONS of little toys and cute things for kids)
- Nail polish
- Ear buds
- Costume jewelry

Copyright © AliBelle, LLC, All Rights Reserved

- Kaleidoscope
- Swiss army knife (obviously age appropriate to the parent's discretion)
- CD's
- iTunes gift card. (even $5 bucks is awesome!)
- Cash
- Make up (age appropriate)
- Bank
- Stickers and temporary tattoos
- Gel pens, markers, crayons, etc.
- Silly Bandz (or equivalent)
- Trading Cards
- Marbles
- Hair ties, barrettes, ribbons, etc.
- Video game
- Silly puddy
- Magnifying glass
- Coloring books
- Slinky
- Bubbles
- Compass

More Stocking Stuffer ideas…

- USB flash drive
- Mini oranges
- Chocolates
- Kindle
- Bible cover
- Candy Cane
- Gum/breath mints

Copyright © AliBelle, LLC, All Rights Reserved

- Lip balm
- Homemade card
- Bookmark
- iPad/Laptop/iPod cover
- Slipper socks
- Toothbrush, floss
- Gift cards
- Games for a Nintendo DS
- Batteries
- Small books
- Key chain
- Fun or joke gadgets
- Yo-yo
- Deck of cards
- Wine/bottle stopper
- Homemade jam
- Mittens or gloves
- Cookie Cutters
- Baking gadgets (small)
- Pin cushion
- Needle and thread, yarn, crochet needles, etc…
- Crossword puzzle, Sudoku, etc…

I hope these ideas get your creative juices flowing!

Copyright © AliBelle, LLC, All Rights Reserved

Copyright © AliBelle, LLC, All Rights Reserved

Frugal Activities

The Christmas season is not only a time to give; it is also a time to spend with your family. Many moms with children out of school struggle to find things to do that are affordable and fun. Below you will find rewarding, fun, and meaningful activity ideas that will build family relationships and a lifetime of happy memories...without going into debt!

Here are my frugal family activity ideas...

Volunteer. Visit an elderly home and read books to them. Volunteer where you are needed. There are MANY opportunities in every community! Again, get the family involved!

Start a Tradition. Each year, have a cookie decorating, gift wrapping or some other contest. Make sure you have some sort of "bragging rights" statue for the winner to keep for the year. There are a few other ideas in this list as well...

Donate. Have the family go through their rooms and closets looking for things to donate to those less fortunate. It will make space for new gifts as well as bless another human being!

Copyright © AliBelle, LLC, All Rights Reserved

Sing-a-Long. This is something fun we do at my care group each year. If you have a large family, this can be quite a hoot. :) Using the 12 days of Christmas song, each group or couple...depending on size of your family gets one part (or two if small family) to sing. It really is hilarious the way each group sings and how it all comes together. We have some real hams in our group that make this a hilarious activity.

Go Caroling. Some neighborhoods do this as a group. Otherwise, start your own caroling gig. Get friends, family and neighbors involved and have fun blessing someone else!

Go Looking at Christmas Lights. Every year, we put some hot cocoa in travel mugs, get a cozy blanket and all snuggle up in the car while looking at Christmas lights around town. We are quite the critics you know–look out!

Attend Church on Christmas Eve. Many churches have a Christmas Eve service. This is yet again, another free activity to do with your family!

Read the Christmas Story. If you can get dad to do this, that's awesome. Make it a big production. Hot cocoa, tree lights on, etc. Then have him read the story of Christmas. :)

Scrapbook Fun. Take last year's pictures and create a scrapbook as a family. Each person gets

Copyright © AliBelle, LLC, All Rights Reserved

their own stack of pictures and pages they can make.

Nativity Fun! You can make one as a family using stuff you have in your house. You can have each member make their own, and even make it a special "bragging rights" contest of who made the best each year. You can also act out the story as a family–or get the kids to put on a show for you. So many options…

Advent. You can find books and info online to help you do your own Advent celebration activities.

Have a costume contest. The rules: Must have something to do with Christmas and can ONLY use stuff you have in your house. Then, vote for who has the best. Oh, and each family member must vote for ONE other member –NOT themselves!

Gift Card Deals. A lot of companies offer gift card deals. You just have to take the time to find them. For example: you can get a $25 gift card for $15. Look online…you may find yourself a great deal!

Make Cards. Create homemade cards and write a special message to the person receiving it. Make it personal and it is sure to be a favorite! This is a great activity to do as a family.

Copyright © AliBelle, LLC, All Rights Reserved

White Elephant. This is always fun. Have a party. Make sure everyone brings a dish to share. Don't break the bank decorating either. Then, have each person bring a gift valued between $5-$20, depending on what you think everyone's budget will be. This is a fun way to get together and receive a gift! I have been to parties with $5 limits and $25 limits. I had a BLAST at all of them! Make the limit what YOU can afford! You can make it a family … or friend tradition. Look up "White Elephant" party on Google for rule variations.

Clay. Use clay to create a nativity scene, ornaments, etc. Kids love to play with clay and play-dough. Let them get creative with the Christmas theme. You can also find instructions online as to how to make your clay creations last for years and years.

Scavenger Hunt. This can be a fun family tradition. Create an age appropriate scavenger hunt for the kids/family. Make it fun, and have some sweet treats along the way. In the end, whoever wins gets to open one present. Make sure you have some small things for the runner ups so there are no hard feelings!

Local Tree Lighting Ceremony. A lot of towns have a tree lighting ceremony downtown. It is a free activity to do as a family.

Copyright © AliBelle, LLC, All Rights Reserved

Make ornaments. Have your kids make special homemade ornaments to give to the Grandparents. Not only is it a fun activity for them, it is a special gift that any grandparent will treasure for life! Or, use them for your own tree!

Fire Pit. If you have a large back yard, why not make a fire pit and have a bonfire on a cold night close to Christmas. Make some s'mores and tell your kids the story of Jesus and why God sent Him. If you do not have a place for a fire pit, just use a grill and pull out some chairs around it! No room for any of this?? Microwave the s'mores, light some candles and have a living room "bonfire". :) **NOTE: always remember to be safe and smart when mixing kids with fire.**

Family Field Day. Do you remember "field day" at school? Create your own family style one. Have sack (pillow cases) races, don't drop the egg, wheel barrel, etc. Seriously, this can be a blast and a new family tradition. If you have a small immediate family, branch out and invite aunts, uncles, etc. Make it a potluck so you do not do all the work, and have a blast making lifetime memories with your kids!

Library. Check out your local library for story time and other free events they have going on during the holiday season.

Copyright © AliBelle, LLC, All Rights Reserved

Let it Snow… I live in the Sunshine State. However, if you have snow in your neck of the woods…enjoy it! Go sledding, make snow angels, and build a snow man–have fun!

Snowflakes. Making snowflakes was always fun as a child. All it takes is scissors, white paper, crayons/markers, glue and glitter!

Track Santa. We do not celebrate with Santa at all, but a lot of people do, so, if you celebrate Christmas with Santa, there is a cool site that "tracks" where he is on Christmas Eve. It is very cute. (www.noradsanta.org)

Christmas Around the World. Our homeschool group used to do this each year. If you can get a few families together, that would be even better. Each family picks a country they will represent. Then you all get together and share several things from your country choice. For example: you will share a little about how they celebrate Christmas, one traditional treat (make sure you give the kids the recipe for it too) and a craft. If you can, get at least 3 families together, that will make an afternoon of fun for you and the kids. Each kid will come home with a recipe from each country, a craft and fact sheet from each country represented as well. This is very fun and educational.

Indoor Camping. If you have a tent, pull it out and set up your "camp site" close (not too close) to

Copyright © AliBelle, LLC, All Rights Reserved

your Christmas tree, and create a Christmas camping experience. If you do this the week before Christmas, you may even let the kids open one gift as a special treat. This can become an awesome family tradition that your kids will love and treasure the memories for a lifetime! No tent? No problem! Make a fort with blankets or just throw some blankets on the floor!

Family Twister. Without breaking a hip, pull out the old twister game and have a blast with your kids. Make it a competition. Whoever wins gets to open up one present! YAY!

Letters from Home. Have your kids write letters to the troops overseas. It will not only make those in the military smile, it will teach your children patriotism and to appreciate the sacrifice they make for our country!

Sponsor a Child. Have you ever seen those trees in stores with names on them? Those are kids that need gifts! I was one of them and someone sponsored me and made my Christmas one year! I was living in a children's home and no one came to visit me on Christmas. I was so thankful…and still am for the person who took the time to get me the few things on my list!

For the Birds. This is a fun activity to do with your kids. Make a homemade bird feeder! Plastic soda bottle, peanut butter and seeds are the basics.

Copyright © AliBelle, LLC, All Rights Reserved

Google the rest. Then place your feeder in an area you can view from inside. Hopefully you will soon have some fine feathered friends come to visit!

Dollar Bowling. Many bowling alleys have a dollar bowling night. It is a cheap way to get out of the house and have fun with the family. However, a nice Wii bowling night will work too! Those are my favorite nights at home! ;)

Candy Cane Craft. We made a reindeer one year, using pipe cleaner for antlers and googly eyes for the eyes. It is amazing what googly eyes, pipe cleaners, glitter and glue can do! Come up with your own creative creatures. have a candy cane craft contest. Sky's the limit, here too, ladies. :) It would also be a great time to share the story of the candy cane....Google it if you don't already know it!

Get Crafty. The best thing about the Internet is that everything is as close as a few key words typed into the search bar. You can find tons of things to do. However, my favorite kid friendly craft site is Kaboose.com They have TONS of ideas to help keep the kids busy and creative!

Visit the Local Zoo. Many zoos are not too expensive for locals. However, if money is too tight for even this idea, visit your local pet store and let the kids cuddle a kitty or puppy. We have one (PetLand) that has fish, kittens, puppies,

Copyright © AliBelle, LLC, All Rights Reserved

reptiles, bunnies, and many other animals. It is a great and free way to kill time!

Spa at Home. Great for Moms, teenage daughters or both! Find some homemade recipes online. Send out a special invitation to a few of your girlfriends and have a spa at home day. You will each bring ONE inexpensive spa item to contribute and one to give away. Everyone should also bring their own beauty stuff to use. So, you will have your stuff, stuff to share and so on. Put each of the items brought to "give away" in a big "grab bag" and at the end of the party draw straws for order, and let each woman pick a gift from the bag!

Christmas Time Capsule. This can be a yearly tradition. Purchase a large and Christmasy box (like the kind you would put a gift in with no wrapping), and every year have each family member put one item in it that represents their year. Then the next year, open it up and enjoy the memory making moments and conversations. Then, repeat it every year! It is an AWESOME way to encourage communication and promote memorable conversation. Keep adding to it year after year to see how life changes. Make sure that you date the items and add a pic of each family member too, or at least a family photo from that year so that you can see the changes over the years. When the kids grow up, Mom will have a box of wonderful memories! (Thank you to my beautiful daughter for this idea!)

Copyright © AliBelle, LLC, All Rights Reserved

Local Events. Many towns have various activities, festivals, etc. going on this time of year. Do a search and see if any fit your budget.

Twelve Days of Christmas Fun! Each day do something fun that relates to that verse of the song. I included a few ideas, but please do not limit yourself to them…you may think of something better!

A Partridge in a Pear: make a pear tart, roast pears or make a pear jam.

2 Turtle Doves: make candy turtles, draw turtles, do some sort of turtle craft, or go to the pet store and look at turtles. (Yes, I know turtle doves are birds, but there are other birds in the song!)

3 French Hens: make your family's favorite chicken recipe. Learn a French recipe that uses chicken or poultry and make it as a family!

4 Calling Birds: go on a nature walk and see if you can find 4 different types of birds–or 4 different birds calling! Do a bird craft.

Copyright © AliBelle, LLC, All Rights Reserved

5 Golden Rings: make homemade napkin rings. I am sure you can find a ton of ideas if you just Google "napkin ring craft".

6 Geese a Laying: make fabergé eggs. Simply poke a small hole in the top and bottom of a large egg. Make sure you allow all of the egg to empty out, rinse and dry. Then decorate with paint, jewels, etc.

7 Swans a Swimming: give the kids a bubble bath, make homemade bubbles and have fun blowing bubbles with them, or go to the park and feed the ducks!

8 Maids a Milking: make chocolate or colored milk, go milk a cow if you have a local farm, read a book about where milk comes from, or just eat milk duds!

9 Ladies Dancing: dance around the house and get silly with your kids to Christmas music, do a dance slipper craft, watch a dance.

10 Lords Leaping: Put on praise music and LEAP in the joy of the Lord. Play leap frog, go look for frogs, draw frogs, read about frogs, etc. Forget frogs and think of another idea!

Copyright © AliBelle, LLC, All Rights Reserved

11 Pipers Piping: make homemade wind instruments. Google; pipe craft, trumpet craft, etc. Watch a band or listen to wind instruments.

12 Drummers Drumming: make a homemade drum, play the drums, use different items to hear the different "drum" noises, listen to the little drummer boy song, watch the little drummer boy...

Copyright © AliBelle, LLC, All Rights Reserved

Frugal Yummies

Let's face it, diets fall by the wayside during the holiday season. Food is a wonderful part of this time of year! Below you will find activities, gift ideas and more related to food, glorious food.

Here are my frugal foodie ideas...

Feed the Hungry. Buy some groceries and donate them to a local food bank. You can also serve food at a local soup kitchen. Doing this as a family will teach your children the importance of caring for the poor. Habits started in childhood stay with us for a lifetime!

Have a Pot Luck. Instead of doing it all yourself and spending far too much time and money, let everyone get involved. It's a great way to try other dishes, bond, and get the family working together to save money!

Share a Recipe. Do you have a friend that has been begging you for a certain recipe? Why not give it to her!? What's the big secret?? Who will have it when you are dead? Spread the love. Write it out on a pretty decorative recipe card and show her how much you love her. Better yet, make it an invite instead...have her over and SHOW her how

Copyright © AliBelle, LLC, All Rights Reserved

to make the recipe! Building relationships is FAR more important than "secret" recipes!

Mallow Men. Love this idea from my daughter! Make snow men with marshmallows! GREAT and tasty activity to do! All you need is large jet puffed marshmallows, white frosting (to keep the marshmallow stacks together), pretzel sticks, and a variety small candies to use. Each person creates their own special mallow men!

Homemade Flavored Oil. Purchase a tall pretty jar. You can find cheap jars in almost any store. Fill it with olive oil and other tasty flavorings. A few ideas: fresh herbs like rosemary, garlic, peppers, etc. Make it a couple weeks ahead of time so flavors are melded well. Make sure jar is sealed tight as well. You can probably find some helpful tips online.

Popcorn Fun. There are so many things you can do with popcorn. Why not make some flavored popcorn balls? Or use them to create cool Christmas characters (you will need a few other items for this…be creative)? Popcorn is cheap and you can enjoy creating and eating all in one!

Make Candy Apples! Yummy! Caramel, candy, nuts, etc. Give some away to friends and family–or keep them all to yourself!

Copyright © AliBelle, LLC, All Rights Reserved

Eat Free Days. Treat the family to a night out to dinner. Just make sure to do it on a "kids eat free" night!

Decorate Cookies. Easy, fun, and oh so yummy!

Make a Gingerbread House. You can either buy a kit, look through some cookbooks, or Google: 'how to make an easy gingerbread house' or 'kid friendly gingerbread house' … or something in that range. Better yet–wing it. That's always the most fun way to do stuff like that. It allows for creativity.

Make Homemade Candy. Peppermint bark is yummy to eat and fun to make. Kids love breaking the peppermint and then eating their creations! This is also a great gift idea. You can put it in pretty cellophane wrap with pretty ribbon and there you have a yummy and fabulous gift.

Copyright © AliBelle, LLC, All Rights Reserved

Frugal Christmas Tips

I hope all of my gift ideas, activities and such have helped you find ways to have a frugal Christmas that will reduce financial stress, and help you to actually enjoy this time of year! But... I am not done! Below are many more frugal Christmas tips to make your life easier and cheaper during the holidays!

Here are some more frugal tips...

Insist on a Price Limit. Some of us have family/friend gift swaps. Set a low price limit that is AFFORDABLE to your family. It really is NOT...or should not be about the price anyway.

Dollar Tree Christmas. I know this sounds crazy, however, things were so incredibly tight for us one year, that we literally ONLY had $15 dollars to spend on Christmas. Period. So, each of us got $5 to spend at the dollar store on each other. It was the BEST Christmas we have had to date. The torch lighter my husband got me that year is my favorite all time gift, and it works FAR better than the more pricy one we received years later!

Make your Own Decorations. Threading old beads, popcorn and/or macaroni through yarn can be made into a fabulous garland. One year, my

Copyright © AliBelle, LLC, All Rights Reserved

daughter cut out two large strips of an old disposable table cloth I got from the dollar store. She made a pretty bow for each of my lamps. The color worked perfectly and it added a nice touch. You can also make a wreath with pine cones and extra greenery type garland. Get your creative juices flowing and you are sure to come up with some great ideas! And, Remember: Glue and glitter can be amazing helps in craft ideas!

Wrap Cheap. Make your own paper mâché type wrap. Let the kids color decorative pictures on construction paper and use it to wrap. Reuse last year's gift bags you received. You can even use old grocery store paper bags or those cute reusable bags they make nowadays. Be creative with what you have…the wrapping goes in the trash anyway!

After Christmas Sales. This is a GREAT time to buy decorations, gifts and stuff for next year's holiday season. You have to plan it though, so you actually have a few bucks to invest. It is worth it in the long run with the money you will save!

Sell your Stuff. This is a great way to earn some extra money for the holidays. Have a garage sale, sell on ebay, put an ad in the paper for big items. Take stock and see what you have that can bring in a few extra bucks!

Shop Online Outlets. Amazon has tons of gifts in many different price ranges!

Copyright © AliBelle, LLC, All Rights Reserved

Garage Sales. You would be surprised the re-giftable treasures you can find at a good garage sale!

Black Friday and Cyber Monday. These are both GREAT money saving days to shop. Companies are competing for YOUR business!

Year Round. Instead of waiting for last minute shopping--Try starting right after Christmas and keeping an eye out for sales all year long. In the long run, you will save money and time by carefully doing a little at a time.

Target Sales. I looooove Target. I find so many fabulous deals by walking the back wall. They put all of their clearance items (some marked down 70%) on the inside end of almost every isle.

Short List. Honestly, it is not frugal to buy for everyone. Shorten your list. Do not break the bank to get everyone a gift! Live and buy within your means. Going broke to give others gifts is not what Christmas is about, and they would not want you to do that if they love you anyway!

NO Credit. Never ever, ever buy on credit! You will be paying more for the gifts! Only buy with cash or a debit card. You will save the interest and have more to spend later!

Copyright © AliBelle, LLC, All Rights Reserved

Take a Year Off! Try a NO Receiving ONLY Giving Year. This can be a real character building opportunity for the whole family, and a great way to teach that giving is better than receiving. It is important to teach our children–and ourselves to be generous. This can really be a memorable experience for everyone!

Only One. We have had years where we could only do one gift each and the price limit was low. Believe it or not, the time spent together far outweighed only getting one gift. You can only do what you are able. Going broke does not help anyone--or teach our kids how to be responsible with money, or how to be thankful human beings.

Save All Year. Recently, my husband and I implemented a strict budget to help us be better stewards of our money. It is also the only way we will be able to survive and meet our bills. While looking at the budget, I was dismayed to see we do not have much, if any, extra most weeks. It made me think about Christmas and not having any money…again…So, we have decided to do what some close friends of ours do…They puts a few dollars a week away…every week…they put it in a "Christmas" box. It can not be used for ANYTHING except Christmas. It just does not exist for any other reason. Period.

When Christmas rolls around, they already have their money and no need to scrape it up… or worry

Copyright © AliBelle, LLC, All Rights Reserved

about if they will have any! Yay! Anyway, we have decided to do it as well, and I am looking forward to not having that feeling of lack, or wondering if my kids will have a Christmas hanging over my head.

Remember, Christmas should not be about going into debt and stressing out about gifts and the hustle and bustle. It is a time to gather together with loved ones, spread love and build happy memories. Never let it become a financial burden!

Have a VERY Merry... and FRUGAL Christmas!

Copyright © AliBelle, LLC, All Rights Reserved

About the Author

Lara lives in Sunny Florida with her husband and their two beautiful daughters. She is a successful Homeschooling, writer, publisher and work at home Mom.

She is also a chauffeur, friend, maid, chef, business owner, writer, lover, confidant, mentor, teacher, seeker, nurse, boo-boo kisser, cat lover, coffee drinker, Starbucks follower, Mexican food addict, jean loving, sometimes loud mouth, opinionated, outspoken, web designer, iphone carrier, a teensy bit anal retentive, chocoholic, Survivor fan, Bible believing, animal lover, reptile and crawly things hating, speed walking, honest, working my way back to skinny jeans, and...One heck of a strong woman! (Among other things)

You can find more of her books here:

URL: amazon.com/author/laravelez

Her Blogs:

MomsofFaith.com (for moms)

bawtptl.com (for wives)

Copyright © AliBelle, LLC, All Rights Reserved

Find her on Facebook:

URL: facebook.com/LaraVelez.Author

Twitter Handle:

@Faithful_Mommie

Copyright © AliBelle, LLC, All Rights Reserved

Copyright © AliBelle, LLC, All Rights Reserved

www.ingramcontent.com/pod-product-compliance
Lightning Source LLC
Chambersburg PA
CBHW060626030426
42337CB00018B/3214